Primary **Maths**
for **Scotland**

1st Level Maths

1A Practice Workbook 1

© 2024 Leckie

001/01082024

10 9 8 7 6 5 4 3 2 1

ISBN 9780008680275

Published by
Leckie
An imprint of HarperCollins Publishers
Westerhill Road, Bishopbriggs, Glasgow, G64 2QT

T: 0844 576 8126 F: 0844 576 8131
leckiescotland@harpercollins.co.uk www.leckiescotland.co.uk

HarperCollins Publishers
Macken House, 39/40 Mayor Street Upper, Dublin 1, D01 C9W8, Ireland

Publisher: Fiona McGlade

Special thanks
Project editor: Peter Dennis
Layout: Siliconchips
Proofreader: Julianna Dunn

A CIP Catalogue record for this book is available from the British Library.

Acknowledgements
Images © Shutterstock.com

Printed in India by Multivista Global Pvt. Ltd.

This book contains FSC™ certified paper and other controlled
sources to ensure responsible forest management.

For more information visit: www.harpercollins.co.uk/green

Contents

Answers
Check your answers to this workbook online: https://collins.co.uk/pages/scottish-primary-maths

1 Colour the flowers in the pots that you think have more.

a)

b)

2 Estimate which set is bigger. Tick the box underneath the set that you think is bigger. Count to check.

a)

b)

c)

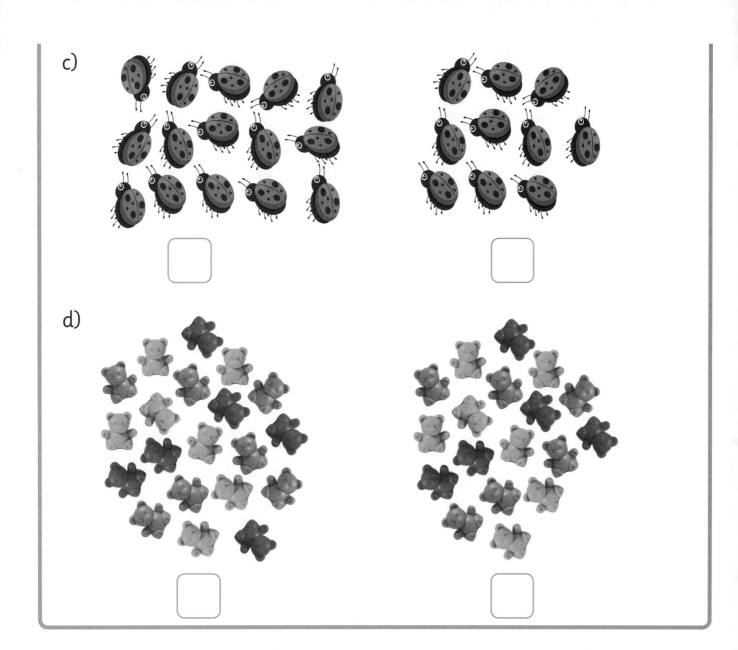

☐

☐

d)

☐

☐

★ Challenge

Isla, Finlay and Amman get cubes to make towers.
Can you estimate who will have the highest tower?

Write their name here:

Count to check.

5

1.2 Estimating and describing collections

1   a) Draw 3 dots on the ten frame.

Is 3 closer to 10 or 0?

b) Draw 7 dots on the ten frame.

Is 7 closer to 10 or 0?

c) Draw 9 dots on the ten frame.

Is 9 closer to 10 or 0?

d) Draw 4 dots on the ten frame.

Is 4 closer to 10 or 0?

2

0   1   2   3   4   5   6   7   8   9   10

Use the number line to help you estimate if these numbers are closer to 10 or 0.

a) 6

b) 8

c) 1

3 Use a ten frame or number line to help you work these out.

a) Write a number that is closer to 10 than 0.

b) Write a number that is closer to 0 than 10.

c) What number is halfway between 10 and 0?

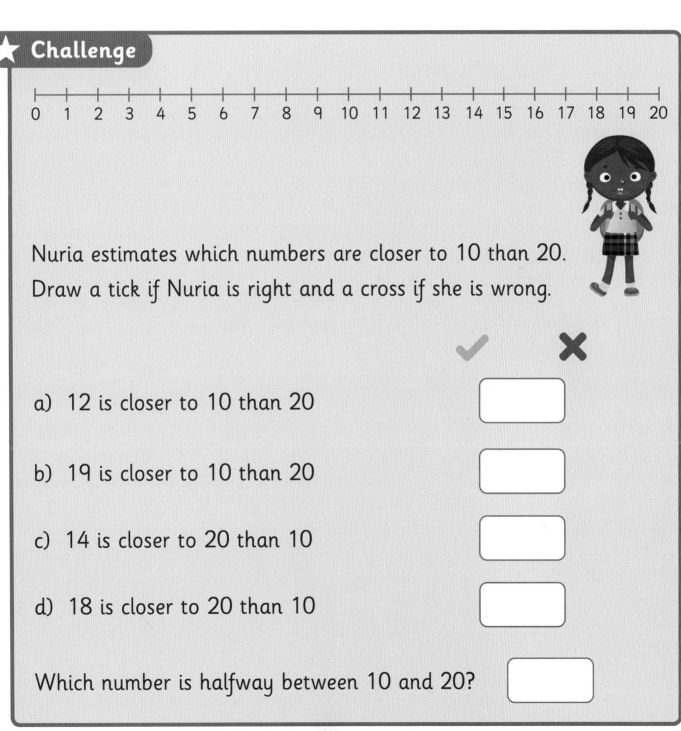

★ **Challenge**

Nuria estimates which numbers are closer to 10 than 20.
Draw a tick if Nuria is right and a cross if she is wrong.

a) 12 is closer to 10 than 20

b) 19 is closer to 10 than 20

c) 14 is closer to 20 than 10

d) 18 is closer to 20 than 10

Which number is halfway between 10 and 20?

1

a) Estimate how many ladybirds are in this set.

Now draw each ladybird on the ten frames below, crossing each one off as you go.

How many ladybirds are there?

b) Estimate how many apples are in this set.

Now draw each apple on the ten frames below, crossing each one off as you go.

How many apples are there?

c) Estimate how many sweets are in this set.

Now draw each sweet on the ten frames below, crossing each one off as you go.

How many sweets are there?

d) Estimate how many marbles are in this set.

Now draw each marble on the ten frames below, crossing each one off as you go.

How many marbles are there?

2

a) Estimate how many dots there are.

b) Estimate how many dots there are.

c) Estimate how many dots there are.

d) Estimate how many dots there are.

3 Estimate how many cubes there are in this picture:

Draw the cubes here and group them into rows of 10.

How many cubes are there altogether?

Finlay estimates there are 30 marbles in this jar. Isla estimates there are 50 marbles.

Who do you think is closest?

 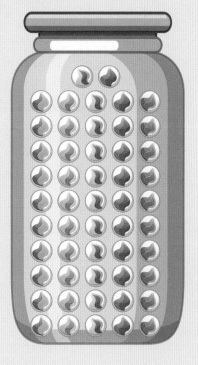 

Explain to a partner why you think so.

1 Can you match each number word to the correct numeral on these t-shirts?

thirteen

nineteen

twenty

sixteen

eighteen

2 Draw the correct number of fruits for each question.

a) Twelve apples

b) Eleven bananas

c) Seventeen grapes

d) Thirteen strawberries

3 How many flowers? Write the number word for each collection.

a)

b)

c)

d)

e)

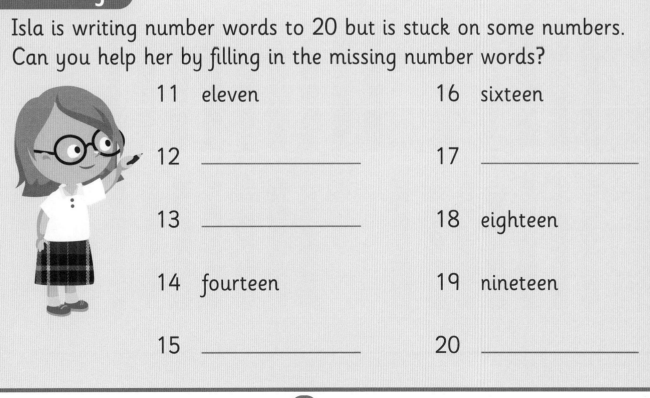

★ **Challenge**

Isla is writing number words to 20 but is stuck on some numbers. Can you help her by filling in the missing number words?

11	eleven	16	sixteen
12	_____	17	_____
13	_____	18	eighteen
14	fourteen	19	nineteen
15	_____	20	_____

2.2 Counting in tens

1 Count in tens to match the bundles of straws to the correct numbers.

60

10

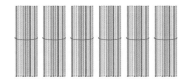

40

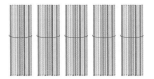

20

50

2 There are 10 cubes in each tower. Count in tens to work out how many cubes altogether.

a)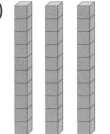

[ ] cubes

b)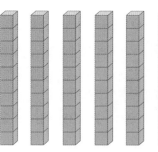

[ ] cubes

c)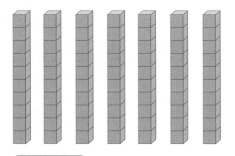

[ ] cubes

d)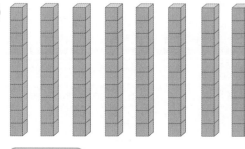

[ ] cubes

3 Fill in the missing numbers on the trains:

a)
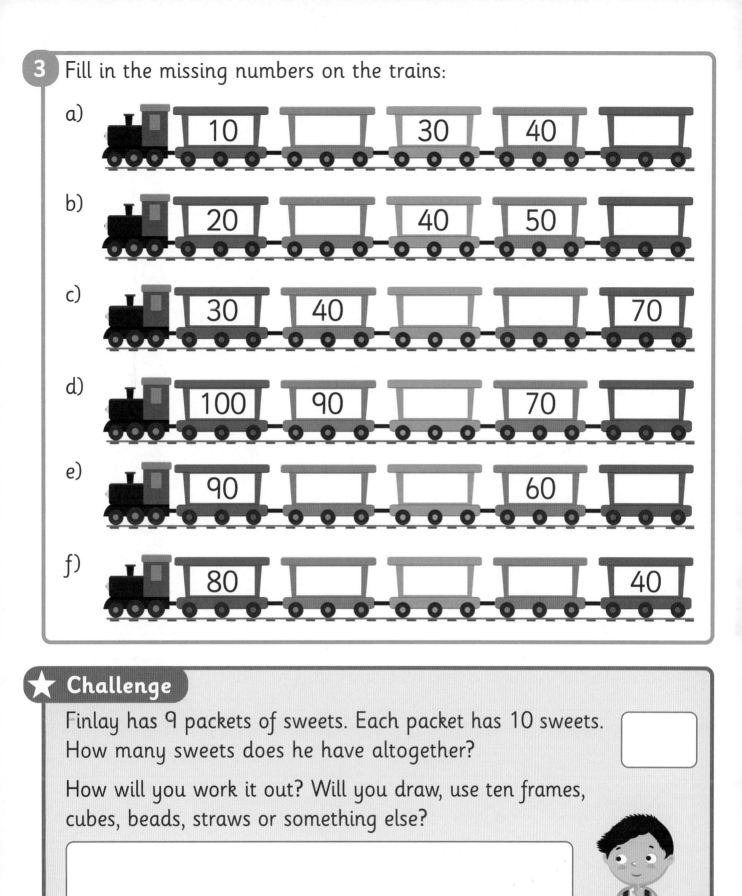
| 10 | | 30 | 40 | |

b)
| 20 | | 40 | 50 | |

c)
| 30 | 40 | | | 70 |

d)
| 100 | 90 | | 70 | |

e)
| 90 | | | 60 | |

f)
| 80 | | | | 40 |

★ **Challenge**

Finlay has 9 packets of sweets. Each packet has 10 sweets. How many sweets does he have altogether?

How will you work it out? Will you draw, use ten frames, cubes, beads, straws or something else?

What if he gives away 2 packets of sweets – how many sweets would he have then?

1 Colour in the flower that shows the correct numeral to match the number word:

a) thirty

b) twenty

c) sixty

d) forty

2 Can you fill in the missing numerals and number words?

10	ten	20	
	thirty	40	
50		sixty	
seventy		80	
90		one hundred	

3 How many dots? Write the number word to match each picture.

a) [six ten-frames of dots] _____

b) [five ten-frames of dots] _____

c) [two ten-frames of dots] _____

d) [eight ten-frames of dots] _____

e) [ten ten-frames of dots] _____

⭐ **Challenge**

The number that comes after **20** is **21**. We write the number word like this: **twenty-one**.

Can you write the number word that would come next?
Try writing all the number words up to 29.

_____

What about the number word that comes after 30?

_____

1 Fill in the missing numbers on this hundred square.

1	2	3	4	5	6	7	8	9	10
11	12	13	14	15	16	17	18		20
	22	23		25	26	27		29	
31		33	34		36	37	38	39	40
41	42		44	45		47	48		50
51	52	53				57	58	59	
		64	65	66	67				70
71		73		75		77		79	
81	82		84		86		88		90
91									100

2 Fill in the missing numbers.

a)

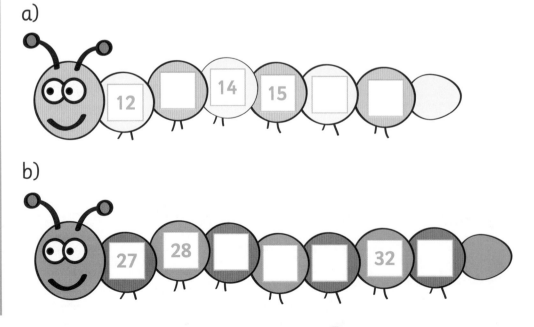

12   14   15

b)

27   28   32

c)

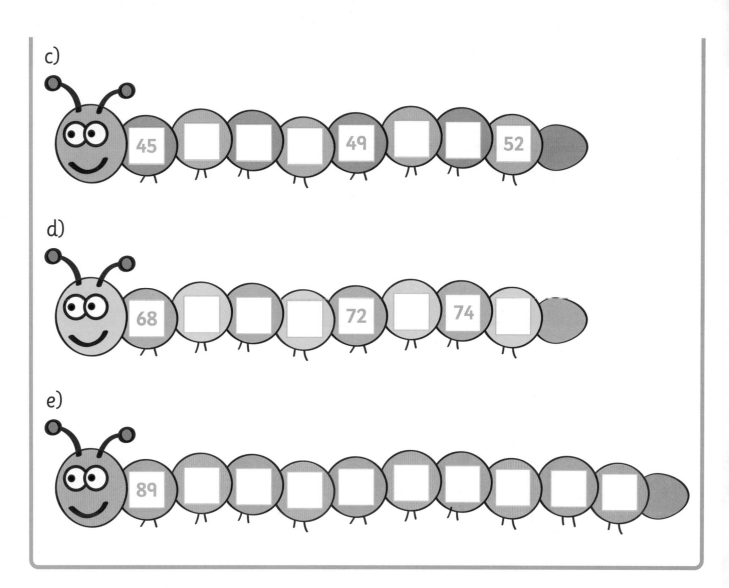

45 ☐ ☐ ☐ 49 ☐ ☐ 52

d)

68 ☐ ☐ ☐ 72 ☐ 74 ☐

e)

89 ☐ ☐ ☐ ☐ ☐ ☐ ☐ ☐ ☐

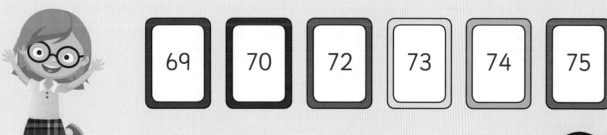

★ Challenge

Amman and Isla are playing a game. Amman has taken a numeral card from the line and moved the cards together so Isla can't see the space. What number is Amman hiding?

69 70 72 73 74 75

Where should the missing card go?

Draw an arrow to show the right place.

2.5 Forward number sequences (2)

1 Write the next number in each sequence.

a)

| 18 | 19 | 20 | |

b)

| 32 | 33 | 34 | |

c)

| 57 | 58 | 59 | |

d)
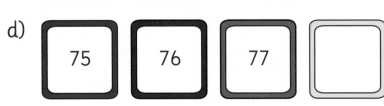

| 75 | 76 | 77 | |

2 Write the next 5 numbers on the number track.

a)
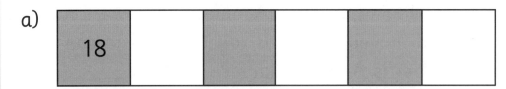

| 18 | | | | | |

b)
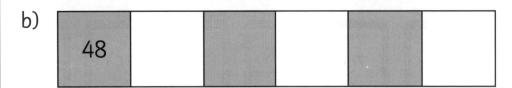

| 48 | | | | | |

c)
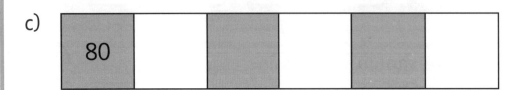

| 80 | | | | | |

d)
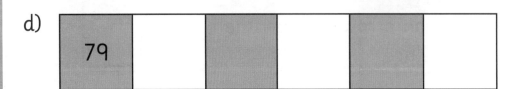

| 79 | | | | | |

3

1	2	3	4	5	6	7	8	9	10
11	12	13	14	15	16	17	18	19	20
21	22	23	24	25	26	27	28	29	30
31	32	33	34	35	36	37	38	39	40
41	42	43	44	45	46	47	48	49	50
51	52	53	54	55	56	57	58	59	60
61	62	63	64	65	66	67	68	69	70
71	72	73	74	75	76	77	78	79	80
81	82	83	84	85	86	87	88	89	90
91	92	93	94	95	96	97	98	99	100

Jump forwards on the hundred square.

a) Start at 23 and take 4 jumps forward. Colour the number red.

b) Start at 41 and take 7 jumps forward. Colour the number blue.

c) Start at 55 and take 5 jumps forward. Colour the number green.

d) Start at 89 and take 2 jumps forward. Colour the number yellow.

★ Challenge

Amman and Finlay play Snakes and Ladders.

Amman is on space number 75 and rolls the dice. He lands on 79. What number did he roll on the dice?

Finlay is on space number 74 and rolls a 6 on the dice. What space does he land on?

Who is the furthest ahead?

1 Fill in the missing door number on each of the houses.

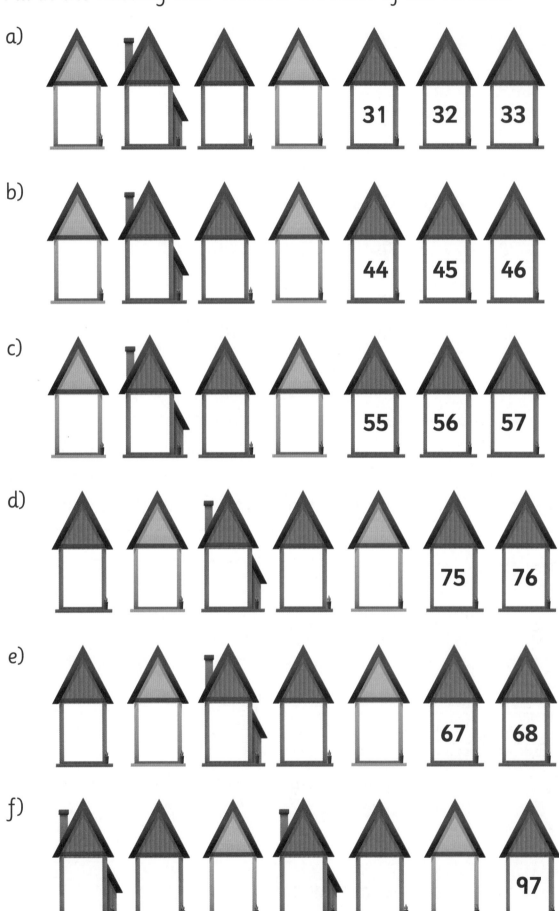

a) 31 32 33

b) 44 45 46

c) 55 56 57

d) 75 76

e) 67 68

f) 97

Count backwards to complete all the missing numbers on the hundred square:

100	99	98		96		94	93	92	91
90	89	88	87		85		83	82	
80		78	77	76		74	73		71
70	69		67	66	65	64		62	
60	59	58		56		54	53	52	51
	49		47	46	45	44	43		41
40		38	37				33	32	
	29			26	25		23		
20			17		15			12	
10				6		4			1

★ Challenge

Count backwards to complete the missing numbers on the number lines:

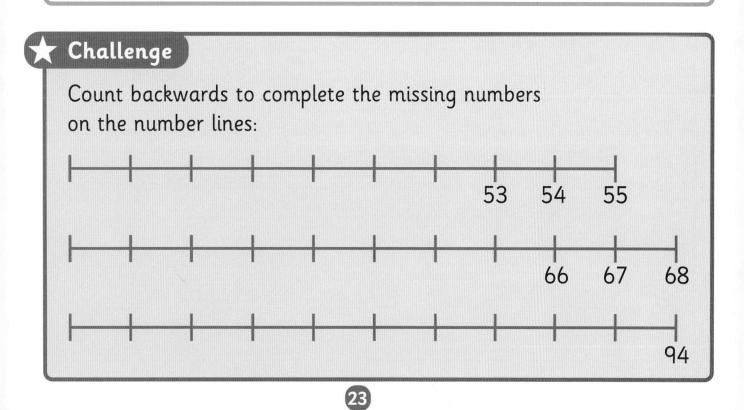

53 54 55

66 67 68

94

1 Nuria is sequencing numeral cards backwards from biggest to smallest. Colour the card that should come next.

a)

| ? | 30 | 31 | 32 |

b)

| ? | 41 | 42 | 43 |

28 39 29 31

40 30 39 42

2 Fill in the missing numbers on the ticket strips.

a)

| | | | | 21 | 22 |

b)

| | | | | 33 | 34 |

c)

| | | | | 41 |

d)

| | | | | 50 |

3

a) 15 16 17 18 19 20 21 22 23 24

Start at 23 and jump back 4 numbers.
What number did you land on?

b) 22 23 24 25 26 27 28 29 30 31

Start at 31 and jump back 3 numbers.
What number did you land on?

c) 36 37 38 39 40 41 42 43 44 45

Start at 42 and jump back 6 numbers.
What number did you land on?

d) 43 44 45 46 47 48 49 50 51 52

Start at 51 and jump back 5 numbers.
What number did you land on?

★ **Challenge**

Can you work out how many jumps from one number to the other by counting backwards?

a) How many jumps from 23 to 18?

b) How many jumps from 31 to 26?

c) How many jumps from 45 to 37?

Compare your answers with a friend. Do you both agree?

2.8 Number before, after and in-between

1 Write the **number after:**

a) 39

b) 56

c) 78

d) 81

e) 93

f) 99

2 Write the **number before:**

a) 30

b) 46

c) 54

d) 71

e) 80

f) 95

3 Write the **number between:**

a)
41   43

b)
66   68

c)
79   81

d)
97   99

4

a) Colour the balloon with the **number that comes after 24** red.

b) Colour the balloon with the **number that comes before 50** blue.

c) Colour the balloon with the **number that comes after 30** green.

d) Colour the balloon with the **number that comes between 39 and 41** yellow.

★ **Challenge**

Can you guess these mystery numbers?

a) Isla is thinking of **a number** that comes before 50 and after 47. It's an odd number.

b) Finlay is thinking of **a number** that is in between 60 and 70. It's more than 66 and less than 68.

c) Amman is thinking of **all the numbers** that come between 88 and 92.

Try thinking up your own mystery numbers for a partner to guess!

1 Isla drew 4 dots then added 10 more. Now there are 14 dots. Count on in tens and write each number in the number box.

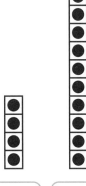

4	14								

2 Count on in tens to complete the missing numbers:

a)

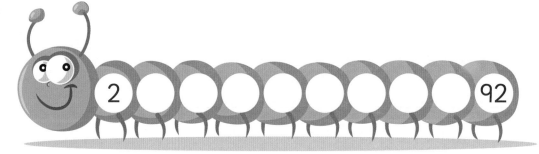

| 2 | | | | | | | | | 92 |

b)

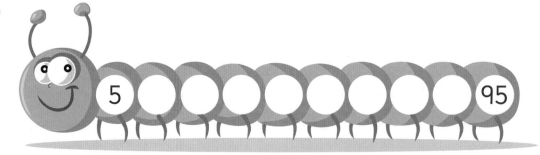

| 5 | | | | | | | | | 95 |

c)

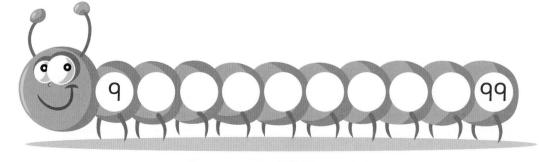

| 9 | | | | | | | | | 99 |

3 Count back in tens to complete the missing numbers.

a)

					73	83	93

b)

							97

c)

							91

⭐ **Challenge**

Amman is counting the money in the class till.

How much money is there altogether?

What if he finds 2 more 10p coins? How much will he have now?

Amman found some more 10p coins. Now he has 95p altogether.
How many 10p coins does Amman have?

2.10 Base ten for teen numbers

1 Count on from 10 to find how many cubes. Draw a line to the matching number.

a)

10 | 4

16

18

b)

10 | 5

c)

10 | 6

15

14

d)

10 | 8

2 Count on from 10. How many dots?

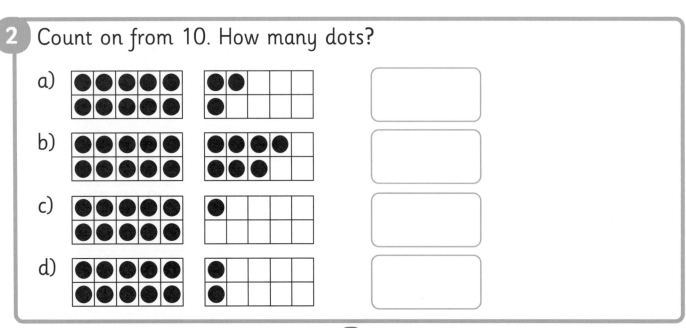

a)

b)

c)

d)

3 This bead string shows 14 is the same as 10 and 4.

a) Draw a bead string to show 10 and 3.

How many beads altogether?

b) Draw a bead string to show 10 and 6.

How many beads altogether?

c) Draw a bead string to show 10 and 8.

How many beads altogether?

d) Draw a bead string to show 10 and 9.

How many beads altogether?

★ Challenge

Isla has one 10p coin and two 1p coins.

How much does she have altogether?

Nuria has one 10p coin and seven 1p coins.

How much does she have altogether?

1 Count in tens and ones to match each collection of cubes to the correct number.

a)

b)

34

48

c)

22

60

d)

2 Isla is sorting the pencils into pots. She puts 10 in each pot but has some left over. How many pencils does she have altogether?

a)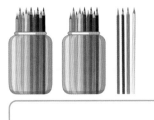

b)

c)

d)

3 Draw the correct number of dots on each ten frame to show these numbers:

a) 25

b) 32

c) 47

d) 98

1 Count in twos to find out how many socks are on each washing line.

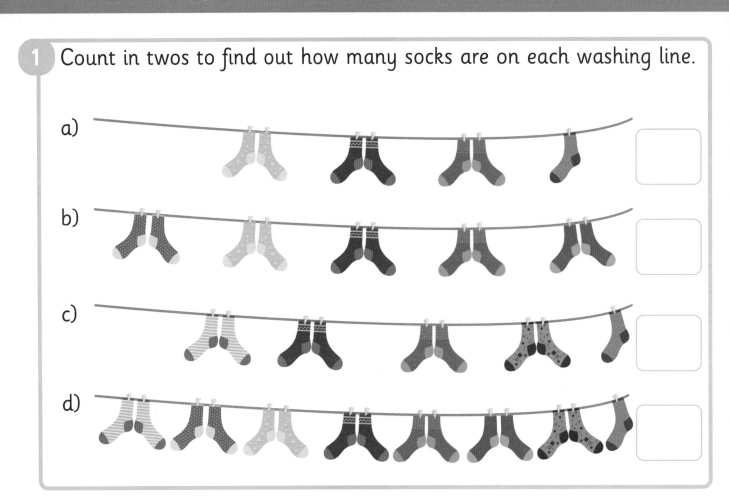

a)

b)

c)

d)

2 Count in fives to find out how many tally marks altogether.

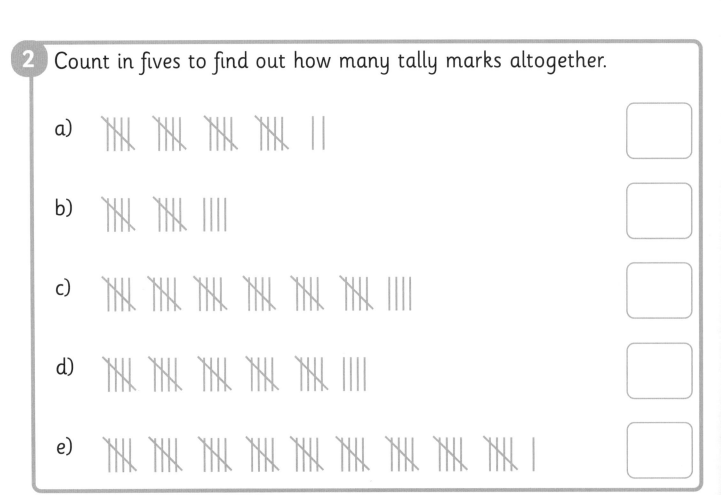

a)

b)

c)

d)

e)

3 Count in twos or fives to complete the missing numbers.

a)

2	4		8		12		16

b)

8		12			18		

c)

5	10		20			35	

d)

15		25	30				

★ **Challenge**

Nuria is helping to sort out all the gloves in the lost property box.

What do you think would be the best way to count them? Draw them here and count how many.

2.13 Ordinal numbers

1 Complete the table.

first	second		fourth	fifth		seventh	eighth		
1st		3rd			6th			9th	10th

2 a) Draw the car that came **first**.

b) Draw the car that came **third**.

c) Write a word to describe the position of the blue car.

d) Write a word to describe the position of the black car.

e) Write a word to describe the position of the orange car.

f) Write a word to describe the **last** car's position.

3 Write the missing ordinal numbers.

4th   9th

Finlay, Amman, Isla and Nuria run in a race. Finlay came **nineteenth**. Isla came next, then Amman. Nuria was in the position **before** Finlay.

Write the position of each child using the symbol and the word.

Finlay

Isla

Amman

Nuria

1 Draw a ring round the addition facts that match each picture.

a)

| 4 + 3 = 7 | 3 + 3 = 6 | 4 + 2 = 6 | 3 + 4 = 7 |

b)

| 6 + 3 = 9 | 7 + 2 = 9 | 2 + 6 = 8 | 6 + 2 = 8 |

c)

| 4 + 5 = 9 | 4 + 4 = 8 | 5 + 3 = 8 | 5 + 4 = 9 |

2 Isla rolls 2 dice and writes an addition fact. Can you write the partner for each fact?

a)

3 + 2 = 5

b)

5 + 3 = 8

3 Write 2 addition facts for each picture.

a)

b)

c)

d)

e)

f)

★ Challenge

Nuria drops 10 double-sided counters.
5 land red side up and
5 land blue side up.

Write an addition fact for Nuria's counters.

Nuria drops the counters again. This time only 1 is red.

How many blue counters can Nuria see?

How many other different ways could the counters land?

3.2 Fact families within 10

1 Amman is writing fact families for these dominoes but has got stuck. Can you fill in the missing facts?

a)

| 3 + 1 = 4 |
| |
| 4 − 1 = 3 |
| |

b)

| 2 + 3 = 5 |
| 3 + 2 = 5 |
| |
| |

c)

| 1 + 4 = 5 |
| |
| |
| |

d)

| |
| |
| |
| 6 − 2 = 4 |

2 Write a fact family for each picture.

a)

| | |
| | |

b)

| | |
| | |

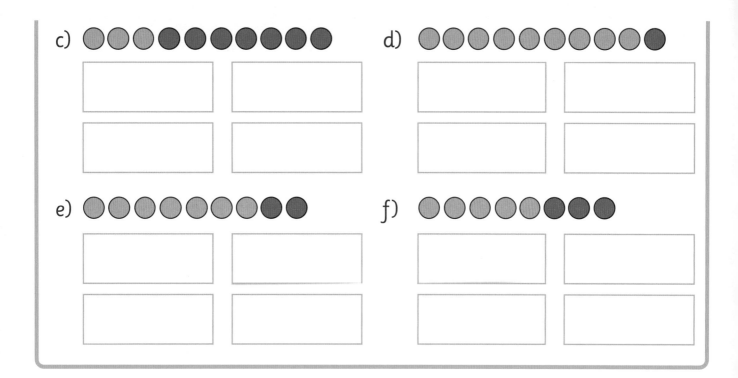

c)

d)

e)

f)

★ **Challenge**

Can you think up a fact family for these 3 numbers?
Write a fact on each part of the Think Board.

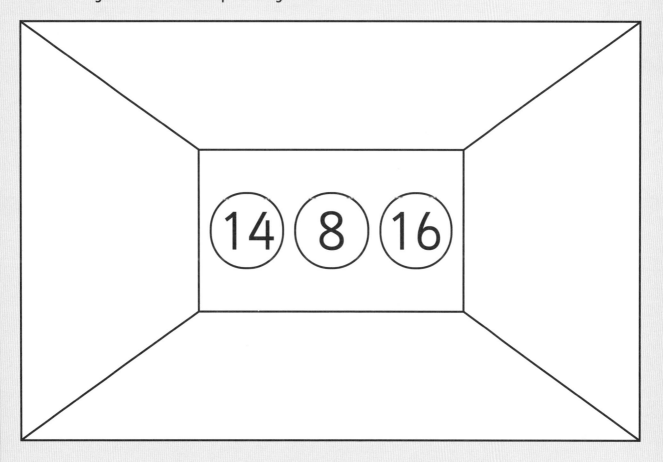

(14) (8) (16)

Try making up some more Think Boards for different numbers!

1 Draw a line to match each double to the correct answer.

Double 7		20
Double 9		14
Double 8		12
Double 6		16
Double 10		18

2 Draw spots on each ladybird to show the double fact for that number:

a)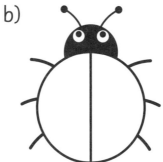

12

b)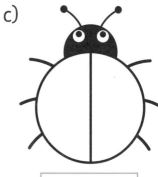

16

c)

20

d)

14

e)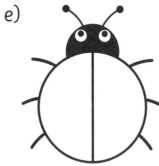

18

3 Fill in the missing number to make a doubles fact.

a) Double 10 = ☐

b) 6 + 6 = ☐

c) ☐ + ☐ = 14

d) ☐ = 8 + 8

e) 18 = Double ☐

★ **Challenge**

Isla is working out 5 + 6. She knows double 5 is 10 so she adds one more to get the answer 11.

Can you use the double facts you know to work out the answer to these problems?

Write the double fact you used beside it.

a) 10 + 9 = ☐ ☐

b) 9 + 8 = ☐ ☐

c) 7 + 8 = ☐ ☐

d) 10 + 11 = ☐ ☐

3.4 Ten plus facts

1 How many straws? Complete the number sentence for each picture.

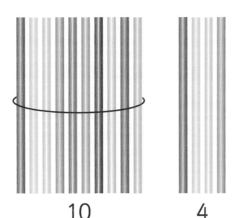

10   4

10 + [   ] = [   ]

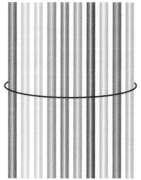

10   7

10 + [   ] = [   ]

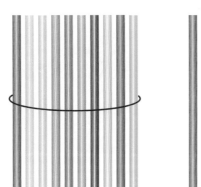

10   1

10 + [   ] = [   ]

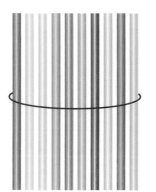

10   5

10 + [   ] = [   ]

2 Draw dots on the ten frames to show these **ten plus** facts.

a)

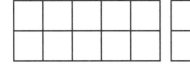

10 + 2 = 12

b)

10 + 6 = 16

c)

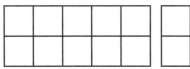

10 + 9 = 19

d)

10 + 3 = 13

3 Write a **ten plus** fact for each set of cubes.

a)

b)

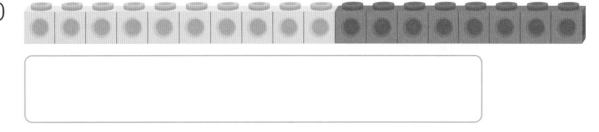

c)

d)

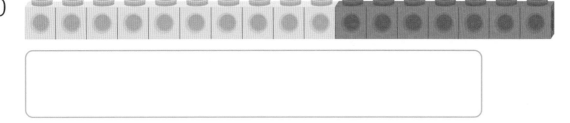

e)

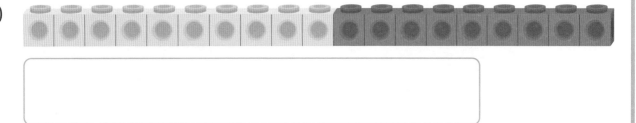

★ **Challenge**

Fill in the missing numbers to complete these number sentences.

a) $10 + \boxed{} = 14$

b) $\boxed{} + 3 = 13$

c) $10 + 6 = \boxed{}$

d) $10 + \boxed{} = 18$

1 Each ladybird has 5 spots on one side.

Count the dots on the other side of each ladybird and add that number of dots to the ten frames.

Complete each addition number sentence.

a)

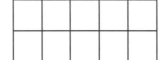

5 + [ ] = [ ]

b)

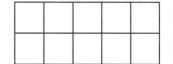

5 + [ ] = [ ]

c)

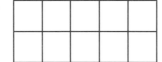

5 + [ ] = [ ]

d)

5 + [ ] = [ ]

2

Colour the balloon with the answer to **5 + 7** red.

Colour the balloon with the answer to **9 + 5** blue.

Colour the balloon with the answer to **5 + 8** green.

Colour the balloon with the answer to **6 + 5** orange.

3 Complete these addition sentences.

a) 7 + 5 = [ ]

b) [ ] + 5 = 14

c) 11 = 5 + [ ]

d) [ ] = 5 + 8

★ **Challenge**

Isla has 14 counters.

5 of the counters are blue and the rest are red.

How many red counters are there?

[ ]

3.6 Addition bonds to 20

1 Work out the answers by making 10.

a)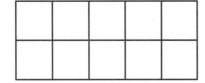

8 + 6 = ⬚

b)

8 + 5 = ⬚

c)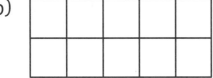

9 + 5 = ⬚

d)

9 + 7 = ⬚

2 Draw dots on the ten frames to help you work out the answers to these addition problems.

a)

9 + 6 = ⬚

b)

8 + 7 = ⬚

c)

8 + 9 = ⬚

d)

3 + 9 = ⬚

e)

9 + 7 = ⬚

3 Work out the answers to these addition problems by making 10. You could use ten frames or a bead string to help you.

a) 8 + 3 = [ ]

b) 6 + 9 = [ ]

c) 4 + 8 = [ ]

d) 7 + 8 = [ ]

★ **Challenge**

Nuria has 8 pennies. Finlay has 9 pennies. How much money do they have altogether?

Draw ten frames to show how you worked it out.

1 Isla uses a tower of 10 cubes plus some more to make amounts between 10 and 20.

Use Isla's cube towers to help you solve these subtractions.

a)

11 – 3 =

b)

13 – 4 =

c)

15 – 7 =

d)

14 – 5 =

e)

12 – 6 =

f)

16 – 7 =

2 Partition the second number to work out the answer.

a)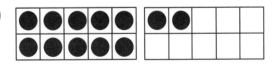

12 – 4 =

b)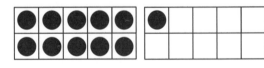

11 – 4 =

c)

13 – 5 =

d)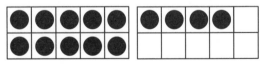

14 – 6 =

e)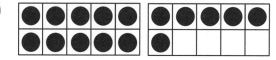

16 – 9 =

f)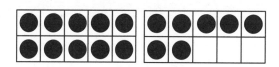

17 – 8 =

★ Challenge

Isla has worked out these problems.

Circle a tick if she got the correct answer or a cross if she got it wrong.

a) 11 – 7 = 3 ✓ ✗

b) 14 – 8 = 6 ✓ ✗

c) 12 – 3 = 9 ✓ ✗

d) 17 – 9 = 9 ✓ ✗

For those Isla got wrong, write the number sentence with the correct answer here:

1 Colour the flower the bee lands on.

a) Start at 11 and count on 3.

b) Start at 13 and count on 4.

2 Count on to add. Draw jumps on the caterpillar to help you.

a)

15 + 2 = ☐

b)

14 + 4 = ☐

c)

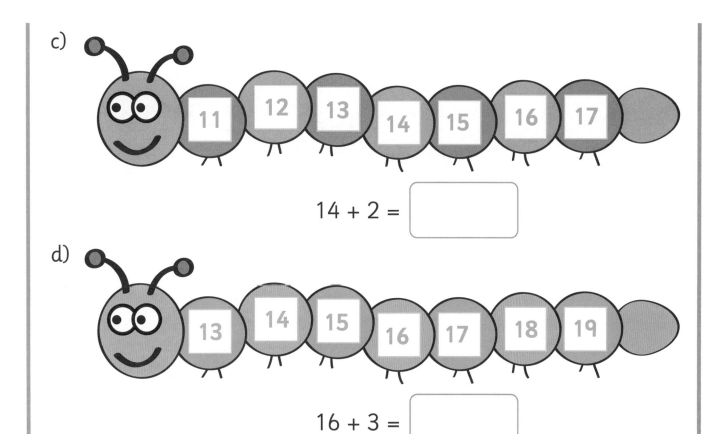

14 + 2 =

d)

16 + 3 =

3 Colour the t-shirt the bird rests on.

a) Start at 15 and count back 3.

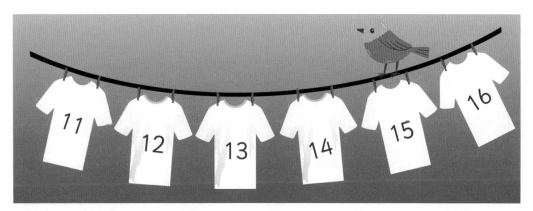

b) Start at 14 and count back 4.

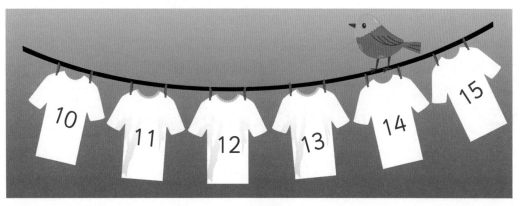

c) Start at 16 and count back 2.

d) Start at 17 and count back 3.

4) Count back to subtract. Draw jumps on the caterpillar to help you.

a)

$$19 - 3 = \boxed{}$$

b)

$$15 - 2 = \boxed{}$$

c)

17 − 4 = ☐

d)

16 − 2 = ☐

★ Challenge

Count on or back to work out these adding and subtracting problems. You can use the number track to help you.

19	20	21	22	23	24	25	26	27	28

a) 21 + 2 = ☐

b) 27 − 3 = ☐

c) 25 − 4 = ☐

d) 23 + 5 = ☐

3.9 Adding two one-digit numbers using a number line

1 Use the number line to complete these additions.

a)
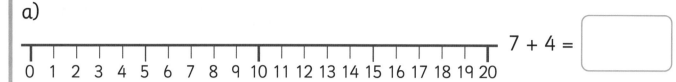
7 + 4 =

b)
6 + 5 =

c)
5 + 8 =

d)
9 + 8 =

2 Use the number line to complete these additions.

a)
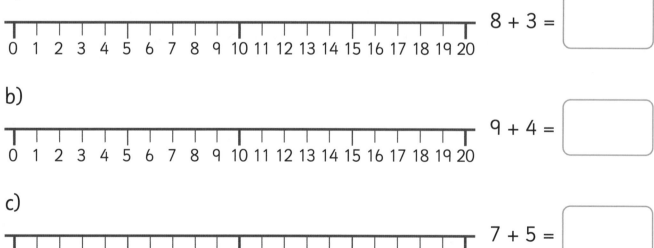
8 + 3 =

b)
9 + 4 =

c)
7 + 5 =

d)
6 + 8 =

3 Write an addition number sentence to match each pair of ten frames.
Now use the number line to find the answer. Draw the jumps
you made.

a)

⬜ + ⬜ = ⬜

```
├──┼──┼──┼──┼──┼──┼──┼──┼──┼──┼──┼──┼──┼──┼──┼──┼──┼──┼──┼──┤
0  1  2  3  4  5  6  7  8  9  10 11 12 13 14 15 16 17 18 19 20
```

b)

⬜ + ⬜ = ⬜

```
├──┼──┼──┼──┼──┼──┼──┼──┼──┼──┼──┼──┼──┼──┼──┼──┼──┼──┼──┼──┤
0  1  2  3  4  5  6  7  8  9  10 11 12 13 14 15 16 17 18 19 20
```

c)

⬜ + ⬜ = ⬜

```
├──┼──┼──┼──┼──┼──┼──┼──┼──┼──┼──┼──┼──┼──┼──┼──┼──┼──┼──┼──┤
0  1  2  3  4  5  6  7  8  9  10 11 12 13 14 15 16 17 18 19 20
```

d)

⬜ + ⬜ = ⬜

```
├──┼──┼──┼──┼──┼──┼──┼──┼──┼──┼──┼──┼──┼──┼──┼──┼──┼──┼──┼──┤
0  1  2  3  4  5  6  7  8  9  10 11 12 13 14 15 16 17 18 19 20
```

Isla has 8 marbles and then wins 7 more. How many does she have now?

Write a number sentence to show this problem.

Use the number line to help you find the answer.
Draw the jumps you take.

0 1 2 3 4 5 6 7 8 9 10 11 12 13 14 15 16 17 18 19 20

3.10 Subtracting using a number line

1 Use the number lines to complete these subtractions.

a)

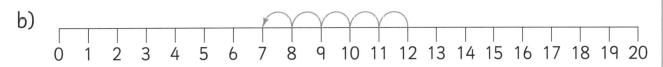

0 1 2 3 4 5 6 7 8 9 10 11 12 13 14 15 16 17 18 19 20

11 − 4 = ☐

b)

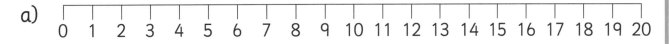

0 1 2 3 4 5 6 7 8 9 10 11 12 13 14 15 16 17 18 19 20

12 − 5 = ☐

2 Use the number lines to help you work out the answers to these subtraction problems. Draw the jumps you take.

a)

0 1 2 3 4 5 6 7 8 9 10 11 12 13 14 15 16 17 18 19 20

13 − 5 = ☐

b)

0 1 2 3 4 5 6 7 8 9 10 11 12 13 14 15 16 17 18 19 20

14 − 5 = ☐

c)

0 1 2 3 4 5 6 7 8 9 10 11 12 13 14 15 16 17 18 19 20

14 − 6 = ☐

d)

0 1 2 3 4 5 6 7 8 9 10 11 12 13 14 15 16 17 18 19 20

$11 - 5 =$ ▢

e)

0 1 2 3 4 5 6 7 8 9 10 11 12 13 14 15 16 17 18 19 20

$12 - 4 =$ ▢

f)

0 1 2 3 4 5 6 7 8 9 10 11 12 13 14 15 16 17 18 19 20

$13 - 6 =$ ▢

g)

0 1 2 3 4 5 6 7 8 9 10 11 12 13 14 15 16 17 18 19 20

$17 - 8 =$ ▢

h)

0 1 2 3 4 5 6 7 8 9 10 11 12 13 14 15 16 17 18 19 20

$15 - 9 =$ ▢

i)

0 1 2 3 4 5 6 7 8 9 10 11 12 13 14 15 16 17 18 19 20

$16 - 7 =$ ▢

j)

| 0 | 1 | 2 | 3 | 4 | 5 | 6 | 7 | 8 | 9 | 10 | 11 | 12 | 13 | 14 | 15 | 16 | 17 | 18 | 19 | 20 |

$15 - 9 =$ ☐

k)

| 0 | 1 | 2 | 3 | 4 | 5 | 6 | 7 | 8 | 9 | 10 | 11 | 12 | 13 | 14 | 15 | 16 | 17 | 18 | 19 | 20 |

$18 - 9 =$ ☐

l)

| 0 | 1 | 2 | 3 | 4 | 5 | 6 | 7 | 8 | 9 | 10 | 11 | 12 | 13 | 14 | 15 | 16 | 17 | 18 | 19 | 20 |

$14 - 8 =$ ☐

★ **Challenge**

How many subtractions can you find with the answer 8?
Write them in the answer box.

Share with a partner how many you found and how you worked them out.

61

1 Draw cubes to help you solve these missing number problems.

a)

6 + ☐ = 10

b)

8 + ☐ = 11

c)

7 + ☐ = 12

d)

6 + ☐ = 15

2 Complete the number sentence by working out the missing number.

a) ? — 8 + ☐ = 12

b) ? — 6 + ☐ = 11

c) ? — 9 + ☐ = 12

d) ? — 7 + ☐ = 13

e) ? — 5 + ☐ = 13

3 Use the number line to help you work out the missing number.

a)
```
0  1  2  3  4  5  6  7  8  9  10 11 12 13 14 15 16 17 18 19 20
```
7 + ☐ = 11

b)
```
0  1  2  3  4  5  6  7  8  9  10 11 12 13 14 15 16 17 18 19 20
```
9 + ☐ = 13

c)
```
0  1  2  3  4  5  6  7  8  9  10 11 12 13 14 15 16 17 18 19 20
```
7 + ☐ = 12

d)
```
0  1  2  3  4  5  6  7  8  9  10 11 12 13 14 15 16 17 18 19 20
```
8 + ☐ = 14

e)
```
0  1  2  3  4  5  6  7  8  9  10 11 12 13 14 15 16 17 18 19 20
```
9 + ☐ = 16

★ Challenge

a) There are 15 diamonds altogether.
How many diamonds are hiding? 7 + ☐ = 15

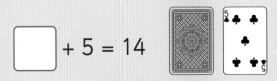

b) There are 17 spades altogether.
How many spades are hiding? ☐ + 8 = 17

c) There are 14 clubs altogether.
How many clubs are hiding? ☐ + 5 = 14

d) There are 16 hearts altogether.
How many hearts are hiding? ☐ + 7 = 16

1 How many dots are on the other side of the domino?

Write a number sentence to show how you worked it out.

a) 9 dots altogether

b) 11 dots altogether

c) 10 dots altogether

2 Count on or back to solve the problems. Write a number sentence to match your thinking.

a) 14 counters altogether. How many under the yellow screen?

b) 16 counters altogether. How many under the yellow screen?

c) 14 counters altogether. How many under the yellow screen?

d) 17 counters altogether. How many under the yellow screen?

3 Use the number line to help you work out the missing number.

a)
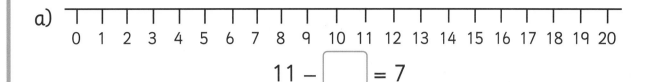

$$11 - \boxed{} = 7$$

b)
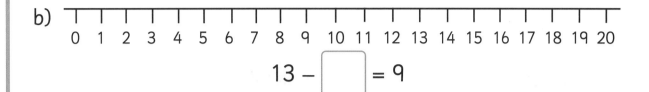

$$13 - \boxed{} = 9$$

c)
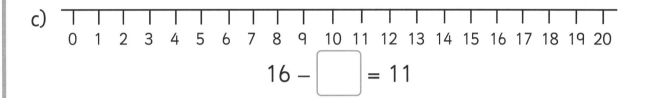

$$16 - \boxed{} = 11$$

d)
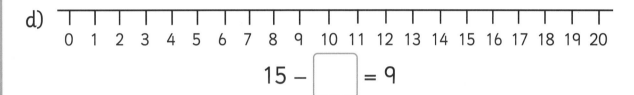

$$15 - \boxed{} = 9$$

e)
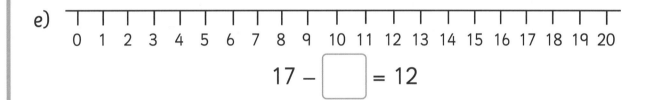

$$17 - \boxed{} = 12$$

f)
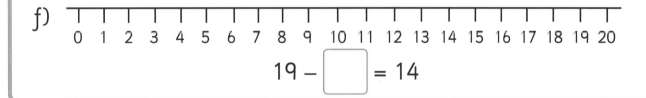

$$19 - \boxed{} = 14$$

★ **Challenge**

Amman and Isla are working out this problem: $8 = 14 - \boxed{}$

Amman thinks the answer is 7. Isla thinks it's 6. Who is right?

Share with a partner how you worked it out. Is there another way you could have worked out the answer?

3.13 Representing and solving word problems (1)

1 Write a number sentence for each problem then solve it.

a) Nuria has 12 red cubes and 5 green cubes. How many does she have altogether?

b) Finlay bakes 11 muffins. He gives 3 to Isla. How many does he have left?

c) Amman has 9 marbles, then he buys 2 more. How many does he have now?

d) There are 18 cars in the car park, then 6 drive away. How many cars are there now?

2 Write the number sentence for these problems and work out the answer. You could use number lines, objects or draw a picture to help you.

a) The pen pot has 7 blue pens and 6 green pens. How many pens are in the pot altogether?

b) There are 11 children at the party. 3 go home.
    How many children are left?

c) Isla puts 8 pink beads and 4 green beads on a string.
    How many beads are on the string altogether?

d) Amman has some grapes. 14 are green and 5 are red.
    How many grapes does he have?

e) Finlay has 17 fish in his tank. He buys 2 more.
    How many fish does he have now?

f) There are 16 children on the bus. 4 get off.
   How many children are on the bus now?

Make up a word problem for this number sentence and share with a partner.

18 + 7

Write down or draw a picture to show your word problem then work out the answer.

Try making up some more word problems for each other.

1 Complete the Think Board for this problem.

I have 8 red bears. Then I get some green bears. Now I have 14 bears. How many green bears do I have?

Write a number sentence	Draw a picture
8 + ☐ = 14	
Objects	**Number line**
	0 1 2 3 4 5 6 7 8 9 10 11 12 13 14 15 16 17 18 19 20

2 Write a number sentence for each problem and work out the answer. You can use objects, pictures or a number line to help you.

a) The class has 19 children altogether but some are outside. There are 16 children in the classroom. How many children are outside?

b) There are 14 people on the bus. Some more people get on and now there are 19 people. How many got on the bus?

c) Finlay had 18 sweets. He gave some to Isla and now he was 15. How many did he give to Isla?

d) Nuria bakes 12 cupcakes. She bakes 6 more. How many cupcakes does she have now?

e) Amman has some money in his piggy bank. His Dad gives him a £5 note. Now he has £14. How much money did Amman have at the start?

f) At the bus stop 10 people get off. Now there are 5 people left on the bus. How many people were on the bus to start with?

★ Challenge

Isla picks 25 flowers.
18 are yellow and the rest are blue.
How many blue flowers are there?

1 Complete the bar models to help you solve the problems.
You can use cubes or other objects to help you.

a) Isla has 9 red pens and 6 blue pens. How many more red pens does she have?

| 9 | |
| 6 | |

Number sentence

b) There are 13 pieces of fruit for snack. 8 are oranges and the rest are apples. How many apples are there?

| 13 | |
| 8 | |

Number sentence

c) Amman makes a tower of 16 cubes. Isla makes a tower of 11 cubes. How many more cubes taller is Amman's tower?

| 16 | |
| 11 | |

Number sentence

d) Nuria has 20 blue blocks and 16 yellow blocks. How many more blue blocks are there?

| 20 | |
| 16 | |

Number sentence

2 Use the bar model to solve each problem. Write a number sentence and the answer.

a) Nuria has 12 felt pens and 9 lids. How many pens won't have a lid?

b) The class vote on what sport they like best. 14 like football best. 9 like basketball best. How many more prefer football to basketball?

c) A bus has 18 empty seats. 14 children get on the bus. How many empty seats are there now?

d) Amman has £15. He spends some money and now he has £8 left. How much money did he spend?

e) There are 19 skipping ropes. 13 children want to play with one. How many skipping ropes will be left over?

f) Isla bakes 18 cookies. There are 20 children in class. Does she have enough to give one to everyone? How many children will not get a cookie?

★ Challenge

Think up a word problem for this bar model:

21	
14	7

Write or draw your word problem here.

Write a number sentence to show how you solved your problem.

Can you think of a different number sentence for this bar model?

4.1 Making equal groups

1 a) Isla has 10 counters. She sorts them into equal groups of 2. Draw a ring around each group of 2.

How many groups of 2?

b) Isla has 15 counters. Sort them into equal groups of 5 by drawing a ring around each 5.

How many groups of 5?

c) Isla has 20 counters. Sort them into equal groups of 4 by drawing a ring around each 4.

How many groups of 4?

2 a) Draw 3 cupcakes on each plate.

How many equal groups of 3?

How many cupcakes altogether?

b) Draw 2 flowers in each pot.

How many equal groups of 2?

How many flowers altogether?

c) Draw 5 spots on each dice.

How many equal groups of 5?

How many spots altogether?

3 How many pencils? Draw the pencils and fill in the missing numbers.

a) Draw 3 pencils in each jar.

[ ] equal groups of [ ] = [ ] altogether.

b) Draw 2 pencils in each jar.

[ ] equal groups of [ ] = [ ] altogether.

c) Draw 5 pencils in each jar.

[ ] equal groups of [ ] = [ ] altogether.

d) Draw 4 pencils in each jar.

[ ] equal groups of [ ] = [ ] altogether.

How many different ways could you sort these cars into equal groups?

Draw them here:

1 Match each array to the correct number of rows and columns.

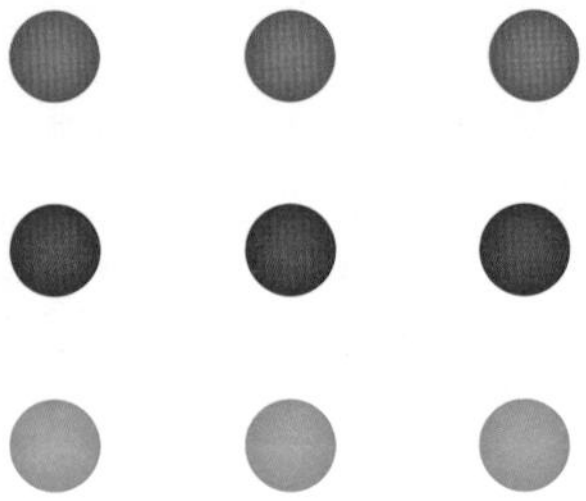

5 rows of 4

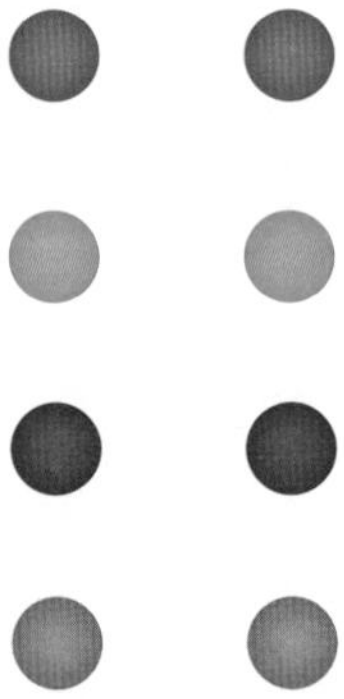

2 rows of 5

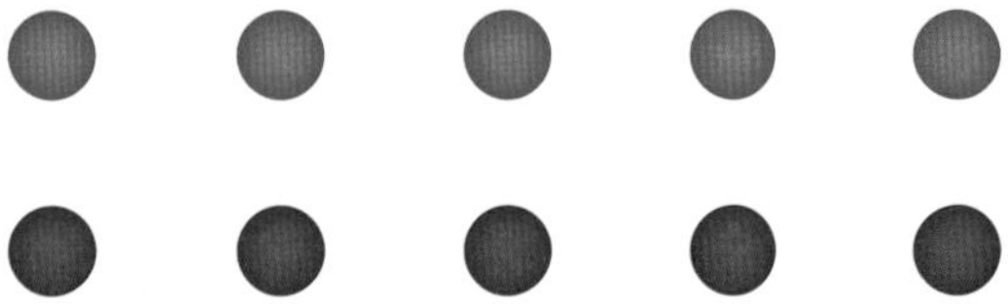

4 rows of 2

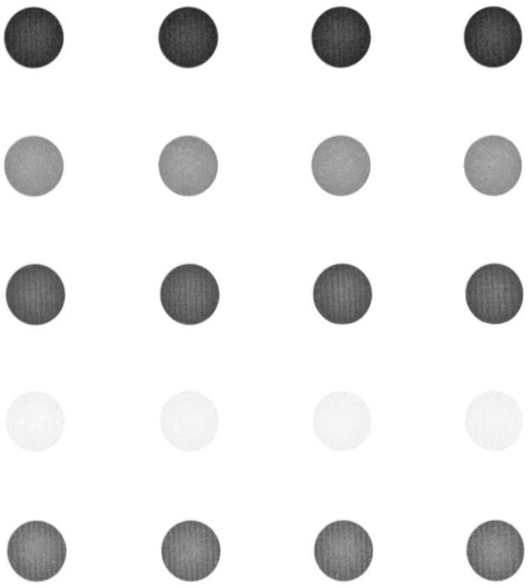

3 rows of 3

2 Draw an array for each question and count how many altogether.

a) 2 rows and 4 columns

How many altogether?

b) 5 rows and 2 columns

How many altogether?

c) 3 rows and 10 columns

How many altogether?

d) 7 rows and 2 columns

How many altogether?

Nuria and Finlay each have 30 cubes. They both make an array with their cubes but each array is different!

Can you make two different arrays with 30 cubes or counters?

4.3 Skip counting in twos

1 Skip count forwards in twos. Fill in the missing numbers.

a)

b)

c)

d)

2 Skip count forwards in twos to count all the socks on the washing lines.

a)

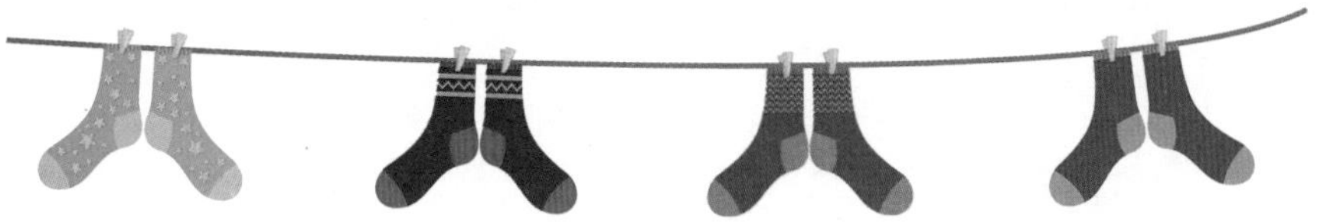

How many socks altogether?

b)

How many socks altogether?

c)

How many socks altogether?

d)

How many socks altogether?

e)

How many socks altogether?

3 Skip count backwards in twos to fill in the missing numbers.

a)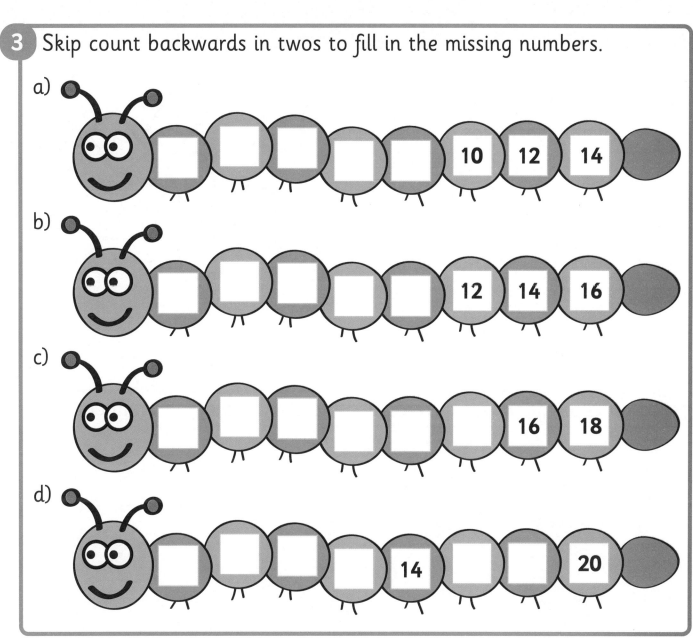

b)

c)

d)

★ **Challenge**

a) Isla starts at 0 and moves 6 groups of 2 to the other side. How many beads does she move altogether?

b) Isla starts at 0 and moves 12 groups of 2 to the other side. How many beads does she move altogether?

c) Isla has 18 beads. How many groups of 2 did she move?

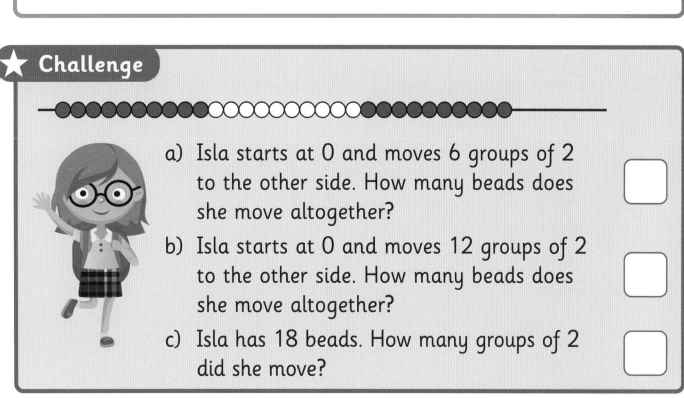

1 Isla has dropped the number cards!

Skip count forwards in 10s to put the cards in the correct order.

Write them here:

30 10 70 90 20 50 60 100 80 40

2 Skip count forwards in tens to complete the missing numbers.

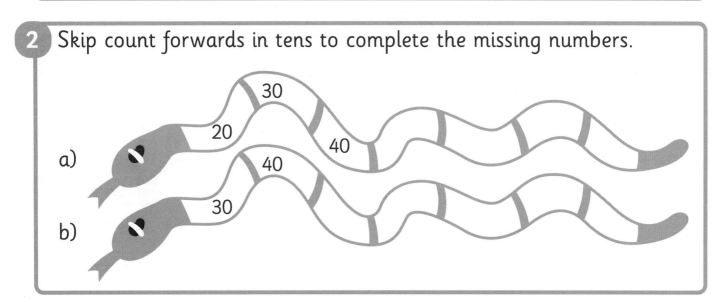

a) 20 30 40

b) 30 40

3 Skip count backwards in tens to complete the missing numbers.

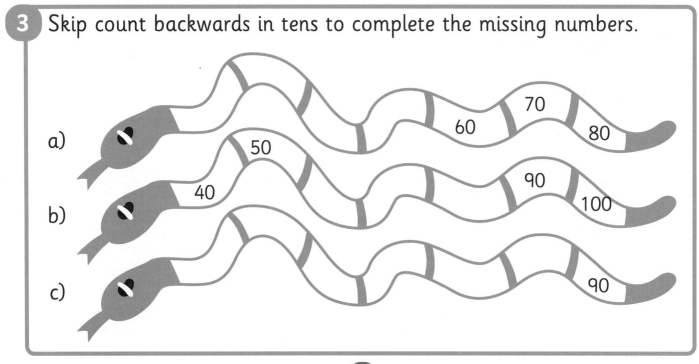

a) 70 60 80

b) 50 90 100

c) 40 90

4 There are 10 pencils in each pack. Skip count in tens to find out how many.

a)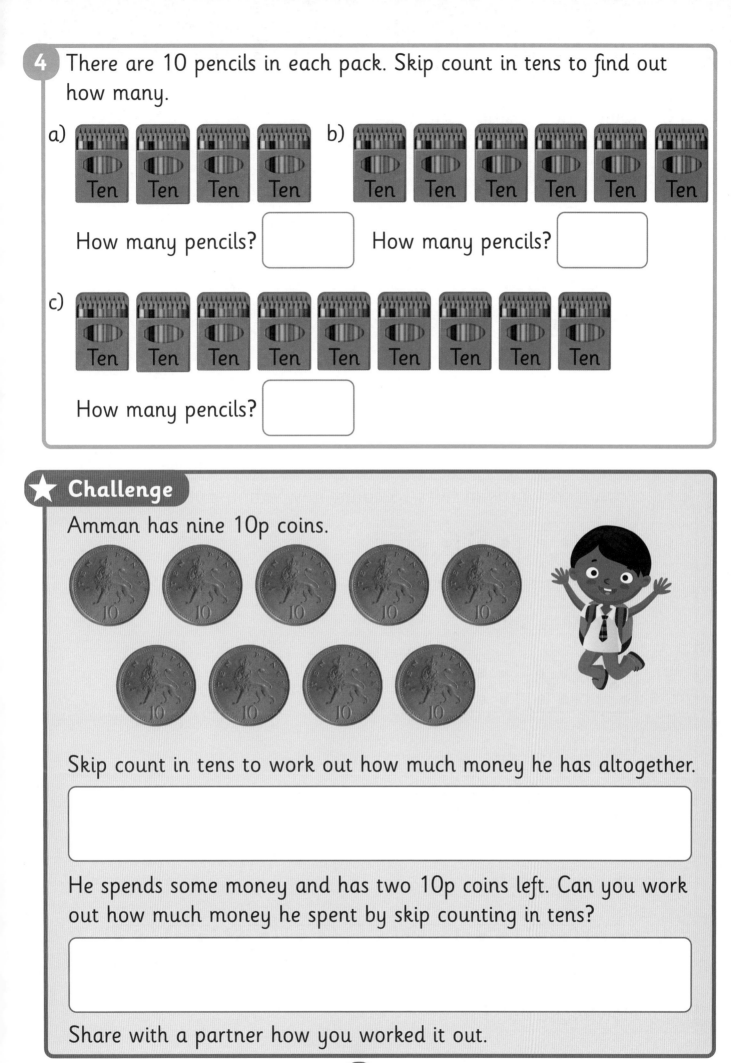

How many pencils? ☐

b) How many pencils? ☐

c) How many pencils? ☐

★ Challenge

Amman has nine 10p coins.

Skip count in tens to work out how much money he has altogether.

He spends some money and has two 10p coins left. Can you work out how much money he spent by skip counting in tens?

Share with a partner how you worked it out.

4.5 Skip counting in fives

1 Complete the missing numbers.

a)

0	5	10							

b)

30	35	40							

c)

50	55								

d)

	20		30						

2 Skip count forwards in fives to count how many dots altogether.

a)

How many dots?

b)

How many dots?

c)

How many dots?

d)

How many dots?

86

3 Skip count backwards to complete the missing numbers.

a)

							35	40	45

b)

							40		50

c)

								60	65

d)

									70

★ Challenge

Nuria and Finlay are skip counting in fives. They count their jumps and colour the number they land on.

Nuria makes 11 jumps and colours number 56.

Is she correct?

Explain to a partner how you know.

1	2	3	4	5	6	7	8	9	10
11	12	13	14	15	16	17	18	19	20
21	22	23	24	25	26	27	28	29	30
31	32	33	34	35	36	37	38	39	40
41	42	43	44	45	46	47	48	49	50
51	52	53	54	55	56	57	58	59	60
61	62	63	64	65	66	67	68	69	70
71	72	73	74	75	76	77	78	79	80
81	82	83	84	85	86	87	88	89	90
91	92	93	94	95	96	97	98	99	100

4.6 Multiplying using skip counting

1 Skip count to work out how many cupcakes there are altogether. Fill in the missing numbers.

a)

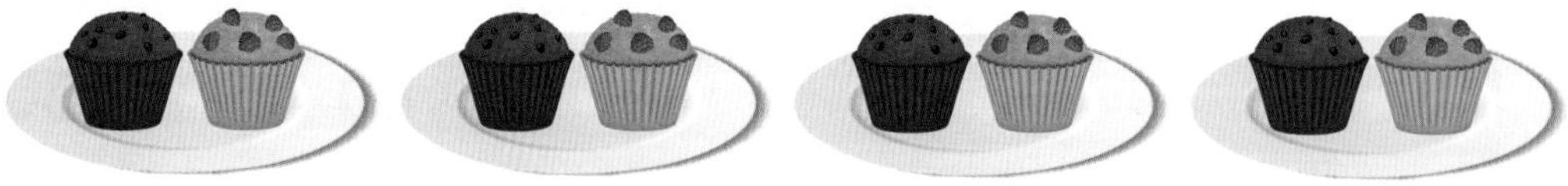

☐ equal groups of ☐ = ☐

b)

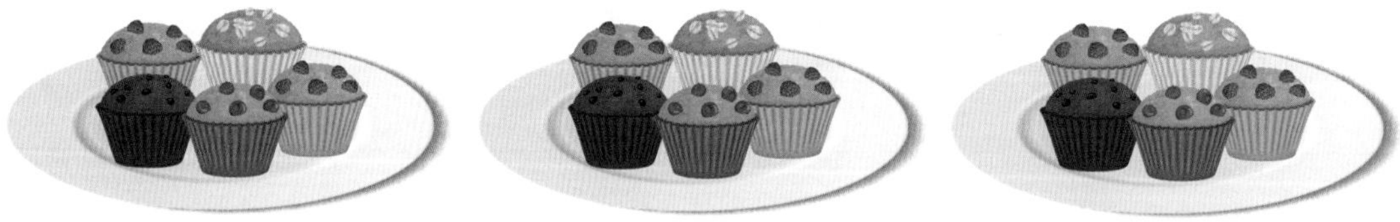

☐ equal groups of ☐ = ☐

c)

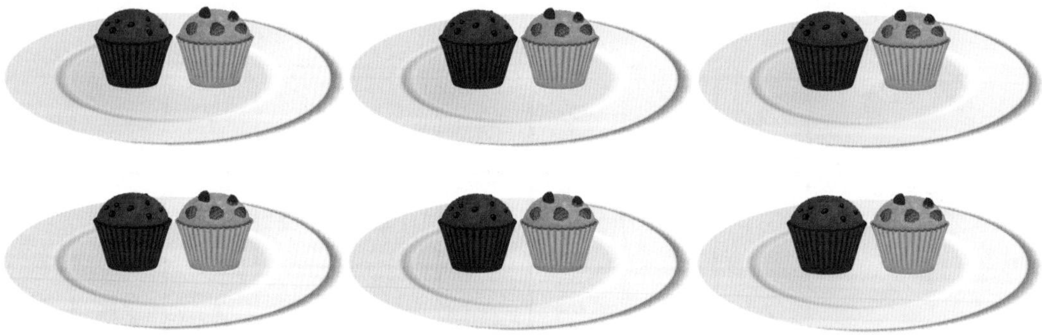

☐ equal groups of ☐ = ☐

d)

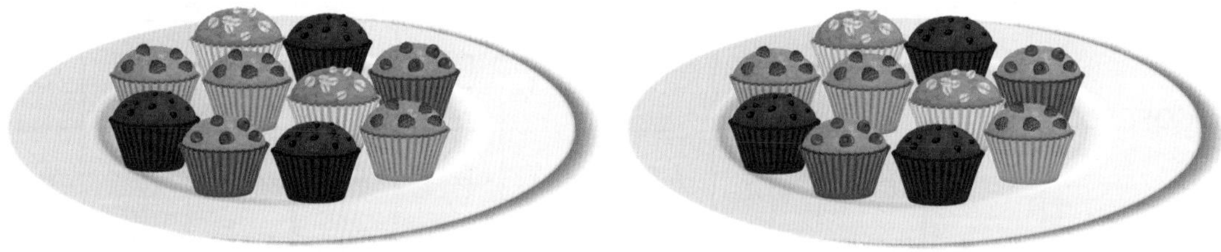

☐ equal groups of ☐ = ☐

2 Skip count to work out how many dots in each array. Fill in the missing numbers.

a)

[ ] × [ ] = [ ]

b)

[ ] × [ ] = [ ]

c)

[ ] × [ ] = [ ]

d)

[ ] × [ ] = [ ]

3 Skip count to work out these multiplication problems. You could make an array or use a number line to help you.

a) 5 × 2 = [ ]

b) 3 × 10 = [ ]

c) 5 × 5 = [ ]

d) 7 × 2 = [ ]

e) 10 × 3 = [ ]

f) 6 × 5 = [ ]

g) 9 × 2 = [ ]

h) 10 × 10 = [ ]

Use skip counting to work out how many cars in each car park. Write a number sentence for each problem.

You could draw a picture, make an array or use a number line to help you.

a) There are 10 rows of cars in the car park. Each row has 5 cars. How many cars altogether?

b) There are 5 rows of cars in the car park. Each row has 10 cars. How many cars altogether?

c) There are 11 rows of cars in the car park. Each row has 2 cars. How many cars altogether?

d) There are 14 rows of cars in the car park. Each row has 5 cars. How many cars altogether?

4.7 Sharing equally

1. Share the fruit equally between each plate.

   a)

   6 oranges

   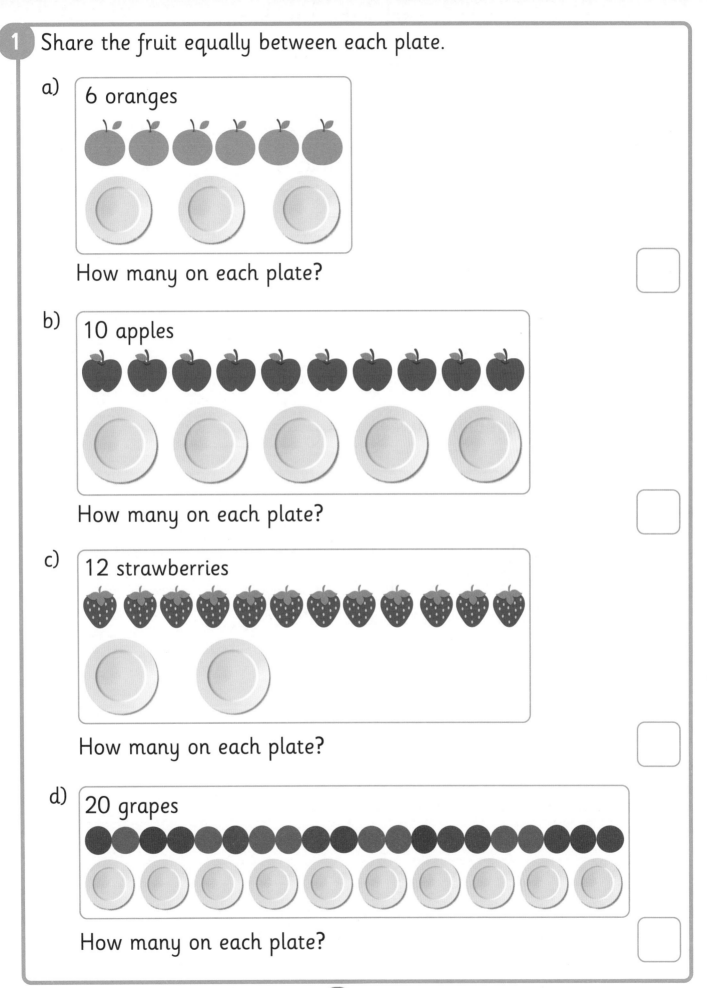

   How many on each plate?

   b)

   10 apples

   How many on each plate?

   c)

   12 strawberries

   How many on each plate?

   d)

   20 grapes

   How many on each plate?

2 Share the marbles equally between the children. Use counters or other objects to help you solve these problems.

a) Share 15 marbles between 5 children.

15 shared equally between 5 = [　　　]

b) Share 16 marbles between 4 children.

16 shared equally between 4 = [　　　]

c) Share 10 marbles between 2 children.

10 shared equally between 2 = [　　　]

d) Share 14 marbles between 7 children.

14 shared equally between 7 = [　　　]

3 Share the cupcakes equally to solve these problems. Complete the missing numbers on each number sentence. You could draw a picture or use objects to help you.

a) Share 12 cupcakes between 3 children.

[　　　　　　　　　　　　　　　　　]

[　] ÷ [　] = [　]

b) Share 8 cupcakes between 4 children.

[　　　　　　　　　　　　　　　　　]

[　] ÷ [　] = [　]

c) Share 18 cupcakes between 6 children.

☐ ÷ ☐ = ☐

d) Share 24 cupcakes between 4 children.

☐ ÷ ☐ = ☐

★ Challenge

Isla has 24 stickers.

If she shares them equally between herself and Amman, how many stickers will they each get? Write a number sentence using the divide symbol to match the problem.

If she shares them equally between herself, Amman and Nuria how many stickers will they each get? Write a number sentence using the divide symbol to match the problem.

4.8 Grouping

1. Sort the sweets into equal groups. Circle each equal group and count how many groups.

   a) Put 15 sweets into groups of 3.

   How many groups of 3? ☐

   b) Put 20 sweets into groups of 2.

   How many groups of 2? ☐

2. Draw the correct number of pens in each jar.

   a) There are 16 pens. Put 4 in each jar.

   How many jars do you need? ☐

b) There are 35 pens. Put 5 in each jar.

How many jars do you need?

c) There are 18 pens. Put 2 in each jar.

How many jars do you need?

3 Make equal groups to work out how many boxes the children need for their cupcakes. You could use counters or other objects to help you.

a) Finlay has 14 cupcakes.
   He puts 2 in each box.

   $14 \div 2 =$ ☐

b) Isla has 24 cupcakes.
   She puts 4 in each box.

   $24 \div 4 =$ ☐

c) Amman has 30 cupcakes.
   He puts 3 in each box.

   $30 \div 3 =$ ☐

d) Nuria has 35 cupcakes.
   She puts 5 in each box.

   $35 \div 5 =$ ☐

Nuria and Finlay have 30 counters.
Nuria sorts them into groups of 5.
Finlay sorts them into groups of 6.
Who has more groups?

How do you know? Draw them here:

Are there any other ways you could group 30 counters equally?
Draw groups here: